Sally Ride

A Buddy Book
by
Rebecca Gómez

ABDO
Publishing Company

Published by Buddy Books, an imprint of ABDO Publishing Company, 4940 Viking Drive, Suite 622, Edina, Minnesota 55435. Copyright © 2003 by Abdo Consulting Group, Inc. International copyrights reserved in all countries. No part of this book may be reproduced in any form without written permission from the publisher.

Printed in the United States.

Edited by: Christy DeVillier
Contributing Editors: Matt Ray, Michael P. Goecke
Image Research: Deborah Coldiron
Graphic Design: Jane Halbert
Cover Photograph: Getty Images
Interior Photographs: Getty Images, Library of Congress, National Aeronautics And Space Administration

Library of Congress Cataloging-in-Publication Data

Gómez, Rebecca.
    Sally Ride / Rebecca Gómez.
      p. cm. — (First biographies. Set III)
    Includes index.
    Summary: A simple biography of Sally Ride, who in 1983 became the first American woman to travel in space.
    ISBN 1-57765-948-1
    1. Ride, Sally—Juvenile literature. 2. Astronauts—United States—Biography—Juvenile literature. 3. Women astronauts—United States—Biography—Juvenile literature. [1. Ride, Sally. 2. Astronauts. 3. Women—Biography.] I. Title.

TL789.85.R53 G65 2003
629.45'0092—dc21
[B]

2002074674

Table Of Contents

Who Is Sally Ride?

Sally Ride was an astronaut. She flew in a rocket, or space shuttle, into outer space. Outer space is very far away. It is where the stars, the sun, and the moon are. Sally Ride was the first American woman to travel in outer space.

Sally Ride

Growing Up

Sally Kristen Ride was born on May 26, 1951. Sally had a sister named Karen. Her father, Dale Ride, was a teacher at Santa Monica Community College. Her mother, Joyce Ride, worked at a prison for women. Sally's family lived in Encino, California.

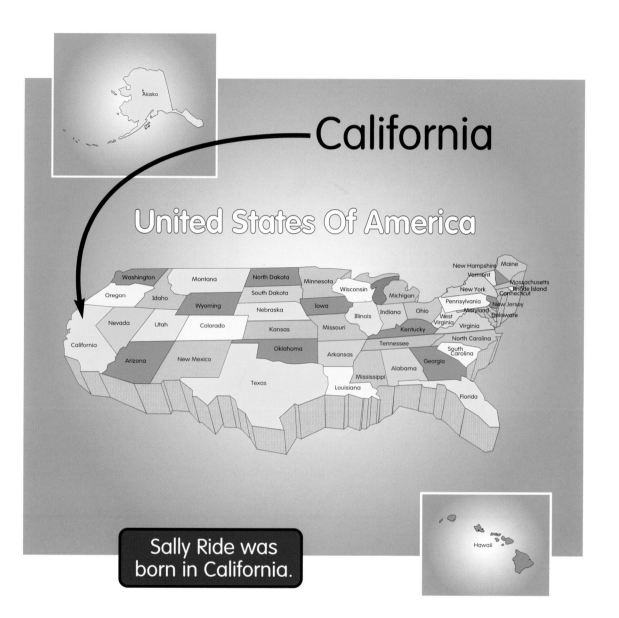

California

United States Of America

Sally Ride was born in California.

Young Sally loved science and sports. Her favorite sport was tennis. Sally played tennis in high school. She became one of the best tennis players in the country. In 1968, she graduated from high school.

Sally grew up enjoying sports and science.

Tennis Or College?

At age 18, Sally Ride moved to Pennsylvania. She went to Swarthmore College. But Sally wanted a career in tennis. So, she left school. Sally began practicing tennis every day.

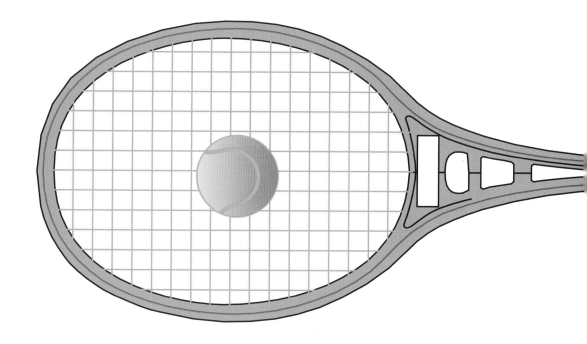

Sally worked on her tennis skills for three months. But she did not want to play tennis eight hours every day. So, Sally gave up on a tennis career. She moved back to California.

Sally started studying at Stanford University. She studied the arts and physics. Physics is the science of energy, matter, and natural forces.

Stanford University

A New Job

One day, Sally Ride discovered that NASA needed astronauts. NASA stands for the National Aeronautics and Space Administration. NASA is in charge of the United States space program. They explore and study outer space.

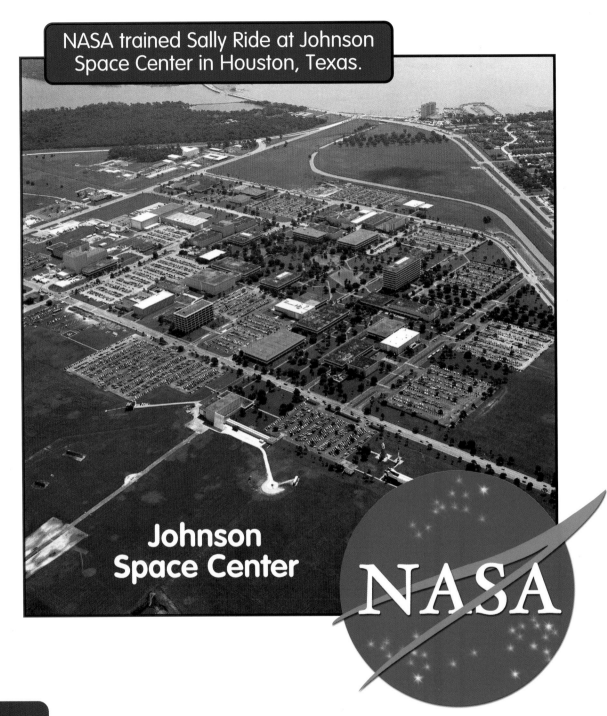

NASA trained Sally Ride at Johnson Space Center in Houston, Texas.

Johnson
Space Center

Sally Ride was a NASA astronaut.

Over 8,000 people tried to get hired at NASA in 1977. NASA only hired 35 people. One of them was Sally Ride. Sally began working for NASA in 1978.

Sally At NASA

NASA trained Sally to be an astronaut. They taught her all about space travel. Sally learned about the space shuttle's controls. She learned what to do when the space shuttle was in trouble. At the end of training, Sally was a shuttle mission specialist.

Sally Ride working at NASA.

Sally's first jobs at NASA were important. In November 1981, she worked in mission control. Mission control helps the space shuttle from the ground. Sally sent radio messages to the crew on the space shuttle *Columbia*. She did this again in March 1982.

Sally Ride worked on the space shuttle *Challenger*.

Sally also worked on the robotic arm of another space shuttle. It was the space shuttle *Challenger*.

Going Into Space

In 1983, Sally Ride became the first American woman in space. She flew into outer space on the space shuttle *Challenger*. Sally spent six days in space. She was the flight engineer.

On June 18, 1983, Sally Ride became the first American woman to travel into space.

A picture of the space shuttle *Challenger* in flight.

Sally rode the *Challenger* into space again in 1984. This time, she spent eight days in space.

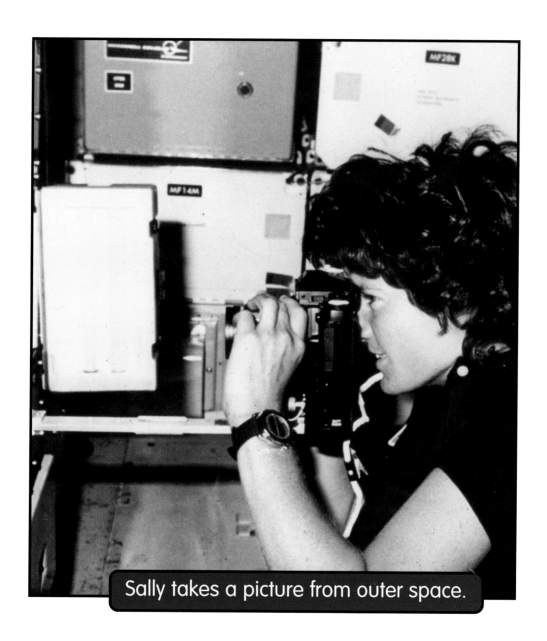

Sally takes a picture from outer space.

Sally was planning to take a third trip into space. But a terrible accident changed her plans. In 1986, the *Challenger* space shuttle exploded. The astronauts on board the *Challenger* died.

The space shuttle *Challenger* before the terrible accident.

President Ronald Reagan gathered a team to study the *Challenger* accident. Sally Ride was a member of this team. She moved to Washington, D.C. There, Sally started NASA's Office of Exploration. Sally also wrote a special report called "Leadership and America's Future in Space."

Sally Ride (right) with other astronauts.

Not Just An Astronaut

Sally Ride was talented as an astronaut. But she had other skills, too. In 1987, Sally Ride left NASA. She began teaching college physics. Later, Sally became director of the California Space Institute.

In 1999, Sally became president of SPACE.com. SPACE.com is a company that offers information about space.

Sally started a new company in 2001. It is called Imaginary Lines. Imaginary Lines has a special club for girls interested in science. It is called the Sally Ride Science Club. It is on the Internet at www.sallyrideclub.com.

Important Dates

May 26, 1951 Sally Kristen Ride is born.

1978 Sally joins NASA.

1983 Sally takes her first trip into outer space. She is the first American woman to do this.

1984 Sally takes another trip into space on the *Challenger*.

1986 The *Challenger* space shuttle explodes upon take-off.

1987 Sally leaves NASA.

1999 Sally joins SPACE.com.

2001 Sally Ride starts a company called Imaginary Lines. Imaginary Lines helps girls stay interested in science.

Important Words

astronaut a person who is trained for space travel.

career work a person does to earn money for living.

explode to blow up.

outer space where the stars, the sun, and the moon are.

physics the study of energy, matter, and natural forces.

space shuttle the rocket NASA astronauts fly into outer space.

Web Sites

Astronaut Biographies
www.jsc.nasa.gov/Bios/astrobio.html
Learn more about Sally Ride and other astronauts.

A Space Library
http://samadhi.jpl.nasa.gov
This web site features maps of the solar system, artwork, and a solar system "simulator."

Index